TODAY'S BALLET

by Rebecca Rissman

CAPSTONE PRESS
a capstone imprint

Snap Books is published by Capstone,
1710 Roe Crest Drive, North Mankato, Minnesota, 56003.
www.mycapstone.com

Library of Congress Cataloging-in-Publication Data can be found
on the Library of Congress Website.
ISBN: 978-1-5435-5442-7 (library hardcover) — 978-1-5435-5446-5 (eBook PDF)

Summary: Learn about the evolution of ballet and today's hottest trends and performers.

Editorial Credits
Gena Chester, editor; Kay Fraser, designer; Morgan Walters, media researcher;
Tori Abraham, production specialist

Photo Credits
Getty Images: Gabriel Olsen, bottom 19, Hiroyuki Ito, top 13, Ian Gavan, 5, Julie Lemberger,
29; iStockphoto: PeopleImages, bottom 15; Newscom: Alexandra Mudrats/ZUMA Press, top
27, Geodakyan Artyom/ZUMA Press, top 11, George Buid/ZUMA Press, bottom 11, Xinhua/
Sipa USA, bottom left 23; Shutterstock: agsandrew, design element throughout, agusyonok, top
19, Angela Royle, middle right, 27, AYakovlev, top 7, bezikus, top 23, 25, df028, top 9, Helga
Khorimarko, top 15, Igor Bulgarin, top 21, julkirio, design element throughout, Master1305, Cover,
bottom right 21, Pavel L Photo and Video, bottom 13, pixfly, middle right 27, Prostock-studio,
bottom 27, ReVelStockArt, design element throughout, Slavko Sereda, 17, StaceStock, bottom 9,
StockphotoVideo, bottom 7, ZenStockers, design element throughout

Printed in the United States of America.
PA84

Table of Contents

CHAPTER 1

An Unlikely Star

Michaela DePrince stands just offstage. She takes a deep breath and waits for her **cue**. The music begins. She lifts her arms gracefully and walks onto the stage. The audience bursts into applause.

DePrince is an unlikely ballet star. She first learned about the dance style when she was a young orphan living in war-torn Sierra Leone. She saw a magazine with a picture of a ballerina on the cover. It looked beautiful and exciting to the young girl. But ballet was worlds away from what DePrince knew. Many people treated her poorly because she has a skin condition called vitiligo. This creates a speckled appearance on the skin. People in DePrince's village said it was the curse of the devil.

When she was 4 years old, an American couple adopted DePrince. They brought her to dance classes when she was 5 years old. DePrince worked hard. She became known for her grace, strength, and determination. At age 17, she became the youngest dancer at the Dance Theatre of Harlem's professional dance company in New York. At 18, she joined the Dutch National Ballet Junior Company and became an apprentice to the main company.

cue—the signal to do something in a performance

Michaela DePrince dancing as Myrtha in English National Ballet's Giselle *in 2017.*

Fact

DePrince does not just dance in ballets. In 2016 she danced in Beyoncé's visual album, *Lemonade*.

CHAPTER 2

Ballet's Roots

Ballet's roots date all the way back to around the 1400s, during the Italian **Renaissance**. The first ballet dancers dressed very differently from **modern** ballerinas. They wore bulky costumes, masks, and heeled shoes. Their dancing looked very different too. Early ballet dancers hopped, slid, and curtsied. They often performed alongside **troupes** of musicians to tell theatrical stories at large royal parties.

In 1553, a wealthy Italian woman named Catherine de Medici married the French King, Henry II. She moved to France and brought ballet with her. It became a very popular form of court dance. Over time, ballet moved to the stage, and French dancers refined moves, costumes, and style. They also named many ballet poses and techniques.

In the 1800s, Romantic ballet became popular. This was a very expressive and **fluid** style of ballet. Female dancers wore calf-length tulle skirts. They danced **en pointe**. They appeared to float across the stage, taking light leaps and spins. Today, *La Sylphide* and *Giselle* are popular Romantic ballets.

Fact
Most accomplished early ballet dancers were male. In 1681, Mlle de Lafontaine became the first female principal dancer.

Ballets in the Romantic style are still performed today.

As the years passed, ballet spread throughout the world. At the end of the 1800s, it became very popular in Russia. Dancers there developed a strict training program. A classical style emerged. Russian ballet focused on proper technique, *pointe* work, high extensions, and precision.

Renaissance—the revival of art and learning in Europe between the 14th and 16th centuries
modern—up to date or new in style
troupe—a group of stage performers
fluid—flowing
en pointe—dance style using special shoes which allow dancers to go up on their tip-toes

Romantic ballets focused on female ballet dancers rather than male ballet dancers.

In the early 1900s, a Russian producer named Serge Diaghilev created a ballet company called the Ballets Russes. It included **choreographers**, dancers, designers, and musicians. The Ballets Russes put on shows that showcased ballet as theatrical art, combining interesting story lines, beautiful scenery, talented dancers, and amazing musicians. Ballets Russes dancers experimented with modern moves, new stories, and bold costumes. Some audiences were shocked and disgusted. Others loved what they saw. The Ballets Russes toured in western Europe. In 1916, the dance company went to America. It gave many spectators their first glimpse of this new Russian ballet.

The Ballets Russes did not last long. It broke up in 1929. But the company was still important. Their performers moved around the world. They took their style of dance with them and taught it to others. George Balanchine was a Ballets Russes dancer and choreographer. He moved to New York and went on to found the New York City Ballet. This brought a fresh, new type of dance called neoclassical ballet to the United States. It was energetic, fast-moving, and used more natural positions compared to its classical counterpart. The style earned Balanchine the nickname "the father of American ballet." Many American ballet companies are still heavily influenced by Balanchine's style.

choreographer—a person who arranges dance steps

Thanks to the Ballets Russes, modern ballets like the one shown here are full theatrical performances.

Balanchine style calls for ballerinas to hold their hands in a claw-like shape, while a more classical hand position is shown here.

Historically, ballet has been a style of dance for wealthy, white dancers. But that is changing. **Diverse** people from all sorts of backgrounds are dancing ballet.

Today's ballet often combines its historical roots with new influences. This makes it an exciting, challenging, and expressive form of dance. Contemporary ballet is a style of dance that combines classical techniques with modern dance. Contemporary ballet dancers must have traditional skills, such as dancing *en pointe*. They must also be able to do things like dance barefoot to modern choreography.

One style of ballet that is making waves is called Hiplet™. It is a mix of hip-hop and ballet. It challenges dancers to combine techniques of both styles into one exciting new type of dance. The dances are paired with modern hip-hop songs. Hiplet creator Homer Hans Bryant believes that this style of dance can help connect today's students with ballet's history. Hiplet doesn't just differ from traditional ballet in its style and music. It also encourages dancers to wear tights that match their skin tones, rather than the traditional pink or white. This change helps dancers embrace their **identity**.

diverse—varied or assorted
identity—who someone is

Natalia Osipova followed the traditional path of a ballet star. She began dancing at age 5. By age 8, she had joined the Mikhail Lavrosky Ballet School. She spent most of her childhood dancing. At age 24, she became a principal dancer at the Bolshoi Ballet.

But Osipova is anything but traditional. She believes it is her job as a dancer to evolve and embrace change. Osipova is known for dancing classical ballet with more drama and emotion. She brings a fresh take to an old style. She also likes to try new things and is not interested in dancing the same moves that other performers have done for generations. She incorporates contemporary moves into classical ballets. Some people think this is a bad idea. They do not like to see Osipova change tradition. Others love it.

Natalia Osipova and Nikita Chetverikov performing in The Nutcracker *in 2018.*

Ballet Philippines performing Firebird *in the contemporary ballet style.*

CHAPTER 3

Becoming a Ballet Dancer

Becoming a ballet dancer is often a long journey. Most ballet dancers begin taking pre-ballet classes when they are very young. The typical starting age is between 3 and 7 years old. Formal training usually starts at age 8. Most young dancers take one to two classes each week. These help them learn their positions, techniques, and style. They are also a great chance for dancers to have fun.

As dancers grow older, they may decide to take ballet more seriously. Some do this because they hope to find a career as ballet dancers. Others might do this to prepare for a specific performance like *The Nutcracker*. Still others do this because they just love to dance. Dancers who want to advance in ballet often begin taking more classes to help them refine their skills and get strong. Depending on the company, by age 14 some ballet dancers are taking between 10 to 15 classes each week.

Not all ballet dancers start training at a young age. Misty Copeland is one of the world's most famous ballerinas. Her training started much later than most dancers.

Copeland had always loved to dance. But her first formal experience with dance occured with her middle school's drill team. When she turned 13, she took a free local ballet class. Right away, Copeland showed that she had talent. A local teacher saw her and invited her to study at her ballet school. Copeland began training with famous ballet companies. She joined the American Ballet Theatre studio company at age 18. She became a member of their **corps de ballet** the next year.

Copeland is not just unique because of her quick rise in ballet. She is also unique because of her race and her body type. Most famous ballet dancers are white and very thin. Copeland works hard to make ballet more **inclusive**. She works with Project Plié, an organization that works to diversify dance.

corps de ballet—the members in a ballet company who dance together as a group
inclusive—more broadly included or welcoming

Fact

In 2015, Misty Copeland made history. She became the first black principal dancer for the American Ballet Theatre.

In The Nutcracker, *a young girl named Clara travels to a magical land accompanied by the Nutcracker Prince.*

Learning the Steps

Aspiring ballet stars have their work cut out for them. They have to learn many skills, techniques, and positions. To make things more difficult, most of the words used in ballet are French!

Some of the first lessons ballet dancers learn are how to perform five positions. These basic commands tell dancers how to position their feet. First position, second position, third position, fourth position, and fifth position form the building blocks for many advanced ballet moves. After learning their positions, dancers move on to other techniques. **Pliés**, **arabesques**, and **pirouettes** are common moves.

After they have mastered the basic positions and movements, dancers can move on to more difficult techniques. One of the most recognizable skills ballerinas learn is to dance *en pointe*. This style of ballet requires stiff ballet shoes. Dancers stand up onto the very tips of their toes during some moves. Dancers usually do not learn this skill until they are 12 to 14 years old. This is because their muscles and bones in their feet need to be properly developed. Dancers who start to dance *en pointe* too soon can damage their feet.

plié—a ballet move where a dancer is bending at the knees
arabesque—a ballet move where the dancer stands on one leg and extends the other behind
pirouette—a ballet move where the dancer spins around on one leg with the other leg off the ground in one of many positions

ballet positions

second position

fourth position

first position

third position

fifth position

Fact
Most ballet classes involve barre work. A barre is a wooden handrail. Dancers use it for stability while doing ballet exercises and stretches.

Becoming a Professional Ballet Dancer

Many ballet dancers dream of becoming professional performers. This is a lofty goal. It takes years of work and lots of discipline. But it is also very rewarding. Professional ballet dancers get paid to do what they love: dance!

Most professional ballet dancers start learning as children. Then a lucky few are hired by professional ballet companies. These are organizations that put on dance performances. One of the most famous ballet companies is the American Ballet Theatre, where Misty Copeland dances. Another is the Dutch National Ballet, where Michaela DePrince dances. Natalia Osipova dances at the Royal Ballet in London.

New dancers are often hired as members of a company's corps de ballet. These performers dance in groups onstage. Corps de ballet dancers often work hard to advance in their company. They hope to become soloists. These are dancers who get to perform small, individual parts. The highest-level dancers are called principals. They often star in performances.

CHAPTER 4

Ballet Performances

What goes into a successful ballet performance? Lots of people and lots of work!

A dance performance takes months of preparation. One of the first things dancers do to prepare for shows is work with choreographers. These professionals think about the story they want the dancers to tell. Then they design movements to tell that story. Teaching their routine to dancers can take months. Choreographers are creative, patient, and good at working with others.

Costume designers also help create ballet performances. They are responsible for everything a dancer wears, from shoes to wigs. Costume designers direct hair and makeup for the dancers. They make sure the dancers' appearance fits the music and movements of a show.

Set designers also work on some ballet performances. They create backgrounds, props, and other elements for the dancers to use. The set helps bring to life the scene for the story.

Costume and stage design are important parts of a ballet performance.

CHEHON WESPI-TSCHOPP

Chehon Wespi-Tschopp was born in Chicago, Illinois. Then he moved to Australia and Switzerland. At age 13, Wespi-Tschopp started to take ballet classes. By age 14, he earned himself a spot at the Royal Ballet School in London, England. After graduating from the Royal Ballet School, he joined the Los Angeles Ballet. In 2011, he danced in a Broadway show called *Come Fly Away*. At 21, he was the youngest member of the company.

In 2012, Wespi-Tschopp competed on season 9 of the television show *So You Think You Can Dance*. He performed many powerful dance routines. He danced so well he was named "America's Favorite Dancer."

Today, Wespi-Tschopp lives in Los Angeles. He has appeared in television shows and films and works as a dancer and choreographer. He also teaches a movement style he calls CheForce. He hopes CheForce will inspire more dancers to express themselves through movement.

Chehon Wespi-Tschopp at a National Dance Day event.

Dress rehearsals are a very important part of preparing for a performance. They're a run-through of the actual performance in full costume and with music and stage lighting. Everyone who works on the show must attend. These rehearsals can be tiring for performers. But they are also exciting. Dancers enjoy wearing their new costumes and hearing the musicians play. Some professional ballet companies even allow audiences to attend dress rehearsals. Others live-stream dress rehearsals for people to watch online.

A big part of a ballerina's show prep involves her *pointe* shoes. These stiff shoes are made from silk, leather, glue, and ribbon. But most dancers alter their shoes to fit or feel a certain way. Some cut the leather sole. Some like to stuff cotton or wool inside the toes. Many glue or sew additions into the shoes to make them more comfortable. It can take hours or even days to get their shoes just right.

Dress rehearsals help dancers mentally prepare for an upcoming performance.

A common way to alter pointe shoes is by ripping out the shoes' lining to make them more flexible.

On the morning of a ballet performance, some dancers sleep in a little later than usual. They do this to feel extra rested. When they arrive at their performance location, most dancers do some light exercises and stretches to make sure they are warmed up and ready to dance. Many eat a healthy snack or light meal. This helps them stay energized through the evening. Then they wait backstage until it is their turn to step out onto the stage. The lights come on and the crowd applauds. It's show time!

Many ballet performances end late in the evening. Dancers are often very tired from their work. They go backstage and take off their costumes and makeup. They put everything away neatly. This helps them stay organized for the next day of rehearsals or performances. When they finally get home, many dancers ice their feet. Then they do some gentle stretches. This helps their bodies to recover from the long hours of dance. Teenage dancers try to get between 8 to10 hours of sleep each night. Adults must get at least 7 hours in order to perform well the next day.

Fact
Many professional dancers eat a balanced, **protein**-rich dinner after their performances. This helps their muscles stay strong and healthy.

protein—a substance found in foods such as meat, milk, eggs, and beans that is an important part of the human diet

A ballerina warms up backstage before her performance.

Yuan Yuan Tan performing with partner Tiit Helimets.

YUAN YUAN TAN

When Yuan Yuan Tan was 10 years old, she was approached by the Shanghai Dance School. Her dad wanted her to be a doctor. They tossed a coin. If it landed on heads, she could become a dancer. It did!

Tan grew up in Shanghai. She joined the Shanghai Dance School when she turned 11. She was a hard worker. She showed that she had talent. She won dance competitions and gained fame. In 1995, when she was 18 years old, she was invited to join the San Francisco Ballet. Just two years later, she became the youngest principal dancer and the first Chinese principal dancer in the company's history.

Tan was one of the first Chinese ballet stars to find success in the United States. Today, she is a worldwide ballet star.

CHAPTER 5

A Professional's Life

Professional ballet dancers have long, tough days. They work hard to put on the best shows they can. Unlike most amateur dancers, professional performers often rehearse for multiple shows in the same day. This can be a very busy, hectic way to dance. Here is a glimpse into the life of one professional ballerina, Claire Kretzschmar, a corps de ballet member at the New York City Ballet.

- 10 a.m.: one hour all-company dance class

- 11:30 a.m.: watches rehearsal

- 1 p.m.: rehearses *en pointe* for upcoming show, *Fearful Symmetries*

- 3:10 p.m.: costume fitting for *The Times Are Racing*

- 6:40 p.m.: arrives at the dressing room to prepare for performance in *Swan Lake*

- 7:30 p.m.: warms up by going through some dance positions

- 8 p.m.: steps onto the stage to perform *Swan Lake*

- 10 p.m.: *Swan Lake* ends; goes home

Swan Lake was first performed in 1877.

Fact

Injuries are very common among professional ballet dancers. Physical therapists help dancers recover from injuries and learn how to prevent them.

Careers in Ballet

When ballet dancers step onto the stage, they look like glamorous celebrities. But many dancers do not earn very much money, and salaries depend on the level of dancer. Corps de ballet dancers at professional companies usually earn between $37,000 and $39,000 each year. In big and expensive cities, it can be hard for dancers to live off of their **salaries**. Principal dancers can make up to $190,000 per year. On top of their salaries, some dancers get **endorsement** deals.

Ballet companies pay for many of their dancers' expenses. They provide them with costumes, tights, and makeup. Professional ballet costumes can be very expensive. A single tutu can cost more than $2,000. Ballet companies also provide dancers with footwear. Most professional ballerinas wear their *pointe* shoes for only one performance. This means they can go through hundreds of pairs of shoes each year!

salary—money paid to someone for work done
endorsement—paid sponsorship of a product that includes appearing in advertisements or on the product

David Hallberg is a principal dancer for the American Ballet Theatre. He has endorsement deals with Tiffany & Co. and Nike.

Fact

Ballet careers are not very long. Dancers who are able to avoid injuries can expect to perform into their early 30s.

Professional ballet dancers are often very thin. This is partly due to the physical demands of dancing. A long day of ballet can burn up to 2,000 **calories**. But some dancers are thin because they feel pressure to look a certain way. Ballet has historically favored dancers who have a specific body type. They are slender, with long arms and legs, a long neck, and a small head. Dancers who try to lose weight in unhealthy ways to fit this image put themselves in danger. They can become exhausted or ill, and they can develop **eating disorders**.

Today, many dancers are challenging the idea of an ideal ballet body. They want people to know that anyone can dance ballet beautifully.

calorie—a measurement of the amount of energy that food provides
eating disorder—a medical issue in which someone has a distorted view of his or her body and develops dangerous eating habits to lose weight

Fact
When Misty Copeland was a young dancer, she was told she did not have the right body type to become successful. She was told she was too short and curvy. Today, Copeland's success in ballet shows that the concept of a "perfect" ballet body is changing.

The Dance Theatre of Harlem performing The Four Temperaments.

MEAL PLANNING

Andreea Olteanu is a dancer at The National Ballet of Canada. She eats filling, healthy meals to keep her energized for long days of dancing. Here is a glimpse into how she eats:

- Breakfast: two eggs, bacon, greens, and cappuccino
- Morning snack: apple and cinnamon
- Lunch: fish, veggies, and kombucha
- Afternoon snack: dark chocolate and nuts
- Dinner: chicken and vegetables

29

Glossary

arabesque (air-uh-BESK)—a ballet move where the dancer stands on one leg and extends the other behind

calorie (KA-luh-ree)—a measurement of the amount of energy that food provides

choreographer (kor-ee-AH-gruh-fuhr)—a person who arranges dance steps

corps de ballet (KOR DEH bah-LAY)—the members in a ballet company who dance together as a group

cue (KYOO)—the signal to do something in a performance

diverse (dye-VURSS)—varied or assorted

eating disorder (EE-ting diss-OR-duhr)—a medical issue in which someone has a distorted view of his or her body and develops dangerous eating habits to lose weight

endorsement (in-DORS-muhnt)—paid sponsorship of a product that includes appearing in advertisements or on the product

en pointe (uhn POINT)—dance style using special shoes which allow dancers to go up on their tip-toes

fluid (FLOO-id)—flowing

identity (eye-DEN-tuh-tee)—who someone is

inclusive (en-KLOO-siv)—more broadly included or welcoming

modern (MOD-urn)—up to date or new in style

pirouette (PEER-oh-et)—a ballet move where the dancer spins around on one leg with the other leg off the ground in one of many positions

plié (plee-AY)—a ballet move where a dancer is bending at the knees

protein (PROH-teen)—a substance found in foods such as meat, milk, eggs, and beans that is an important part of the human diet

Renaissance (REN-uh-sahnss)—the revival of art and learning in Europe between the 14th and 16th centuries

salary (SAL-uh-ree)—money paid to someone for work done

troupe (TROOP)—a group of stage performers

Read More

Bowes, Deborah. *The Ballet Book: The Young Performer's Guide to Classical Dance.* Ontario, Canada: Firefly Books, 2018.

Miles, Lisa. *Ballet Spectacular: A Young Ballet Lover's Guide and an Insight into a Magical World.* London, UK: Carlton Books, 2014.

Van der Linde, Laurel. *So, You Want to Be a Dancer?: The Ultimate Guide to Exploring the Dance Industry.* Be What Your Want. New York: Simon & Schuster, 2015.

Internet Sites

Use FactHound to find Internet sites related to this book.

Visit www.facthound.com.

Just type in 9781543554427 and go.

Index